G.R.O.W. Towards Your Greatness!

Published by
Free Your Mind Publishing PO Box 70
Boston, MA 02131
(202) 251-7746
(202) 889-5056 (fax/orders)
info@freeyourmindpublishing.com
http://www.freeyourmindpublishing.com

© 2009 by Omékongo Dibinga
Cover art by Gemal Woods

All rights reserved
No part of this publication may be reproduced in any form or by any means, electronic or mechanic, including photocopy, recording or any information storage and retrieval system not known to be invented, without written permission from the publisher.

Library of Congress Control Number: 2009902399
ISBN: 978-0-9760056-4-3
SAN: 256-1883

G.R.O.W. Towards Your Greatness!

10 steps to living your best life!

Foreword by Les Brown

G.R.O.W. Towards Your Greatness!

Table of Contents

Acknowledgements 5

Foreword 9

Introduction 12

Step 1: Run towards your story, not from it! 14

Step 2: Ask for what you want out of life!..................24

Step 3: Always reinvent yourself! 29

Step 4: Value yourself and your work! 36

Step 5: Keep friends close and enemies far away! .42

Step 6: Perfection IS procrastination! 48

Step 7: Learn money management............................53

Step 8: Make Sacrifices 59

Step 9: Quit your job today! 64

Step 10: G.R.O.W.! 70

Other products from Free Your Mind Publishing 82

G.R.O.W. Towards Your Greatness!

Acknowledgements

  The older I get, the more I understand the importance of saying thank you. We live in a society where the majority of us take and take. It is usually during times of great tragedy that we see the majority of us pulling together. I guess it's only natural. What I am trying to make natural in my life is my capacity to show appreciation to those that matter to me.
  I would first like to thank the Creator for making all things possible. I do believe, at the end of the day, that we were all created by the same source though we have given It, Her, or Him different names. Having lived a life defined by resistance, I am now intent on living a life in search of acceptance and finding common ground.
  I also have to say a heartfelt asantini sana ("thank you very much" in Swahili) to my parents, Dr. Ngolela wa Kabongo and Dr. Dibinga wa Said. You taught me how to be proud of my ancestry and to respect the cultural heritage of others. I hope that I have honored that for you have set a high standard to live up to!
  To my brothers and sisters Said (that film dude), Musau (the closer), Muadi (the general), Shaumba (the artist formerly known as "Yandje"), Kabongo (#88 Kaydee), Pata (Bruce Lee-roy), Simba (the artist still known as "The Chef"), and Moumié (Mr. Last but not least), what can I really say? There are not enough pages here to write what we have

been through as a little African village in America. I think we can say that the ride has been amazing with all of its ups and downs. There is nowhere left for us to go but up! If it was not for you all, I simply would not be alive. I am working hard every day to make sure your investments were not in vain.

To Oprah Winfrey, our paths have crossed more than you know and we have never met. Your standards for living your best life are second to none and as your 30-something year old twin, I will carry on your legacy of loving, living, and giving.

To Dr. Maya Angelou and Dr. Nikki Giovanni, thank you for inspiring me before you knew me and even more after you met me. Dr. Angelou, my rap name is "Young M.A.Y.A.-the Mighty African Youth Advocate." I will continue to try and honor your legacy in everything I do. To Dr. Giovanni, thank you for telling me my country of ancestry was beautiful when only my parents told me so. To Amiri and Amina Baraka, I thank you for simply believing in my potential. To the Last Poets, I say thank you for your continual investment in me and my peers.

Many people have and are still helping me on my path to inner peace and outer common ground. I apologize for any names forgotten in this brief moment, but I have to say thank you to Safiya Songhai, Allyssa Kiser, Ruth Inniss, Nicole Lindsey, Dr. Julie van Putten, Star Bobatoon, Thom Winninger, Vince Toran, Kate Holgate, Vernice Armour, and Valorie Parker. I also would like to say a very special thanks to all of my colleagues, friends and family in Toastmasters and the National Speakers Association (way too many to mention here).

To Les Brown, I can say many things actually, but let me make it simple. My parents taught me that I'm a king. My siblings taught me that in this society, we're still mentally enslaved. My wife gave me permission to escape the plantation of the mind, and you set me free. Thank you for helping me realize that I also possess (as we all do) the ability to be great!

To my wonderful wife, Kendra. We have been together since the junior prom back in 1994. I thank you for finally realizing you could not do any worse in a husband and tying the knot in 2003. We are going on 15 years together and it really still feels like five in my eyes. We have traveled the world, started (and closed) businesses, and have produced beautiful children. I want you to know that all I am doing has been made possible by your undying support of me and my dreams, which have become our dreams. I hope that I can continue to show the same love and appreciation for you as you have shown me. The next 15 years are truly going to be something to watch so enjoy the ride, my love!

To my princesses, Ngolela and Ndeji. I truly did not understand life until you came into our world. You are my breath and my tears, my hopes and my fears. The fear of you not living in a world where you can realize your fullest potential is what drives me and you are the reason I will never go back to the plantation. I cannot wait to live in the world that you are going to create! May society allow you to live a life of trust before suspicion and acceptance over

Introduction

The first title of this book was going to be Managed Coincidences: preparing yourself for a life of greatness. It was inspired from a speech I heard from Dr. Wayne Dyer, one of the world leaders on self transformation and motivation. In this speech, Dyer spoke about how we have taken the word "coincidence" and changed its definition. He asserted that in math, this word applies to two lines that come together perfectly to form an angle, however, we have made the word mean something that happens unintentionally or is unplanned.
In short, Dyer's assertion is that there is nothing coincidental about the word "coincidence"!
This being stated, he then spoke on how we can manage the things that transpire in our lives so that we can create our best life possible. We can indeed make the two (and often more) lines or paths that we are on in life intersect to create our best life! Though I have changed the title to incorporate some of my newer learnings, the underlying philosophy is the same. As you read this testimony on how I have managed some of the coincidences in my life and how many other famous and not so famous people managed theirs, I want you to start managing your own coincidences. I encourage you to look at each of the 10 steps put forth in this book and be honest with yourself about how you will remove all negative barriers to your growth personally or professionally. So often in our lives, we attend trainings or conferences and leave

thinking that we have learned nothing and have wasted our time. We often lament over the loss of funds and return home unfulfilled. I want you to approach such events differently and begin to take a new approach in life. Use this book to launch the space shuttle that is you for you are on a trajectory to fly beyond the stars. Begin today to prepare for the greatness that is inside of you waiting to burst out!

    Look at each step and know that with each accomplishment, you are taking another step on the stairs of success—a success defined by you and no one else. When Les Brown, one of the world's leading motivational speakers over the last 20 years, speaks of becoming a millionaire, he is speaking more of a mindset than the money. As he states, being a millionaire means doing things that make you feel like a millionaire. It could mean getting your first house or a house for your parents. It could mean going back to school when you're in your seventies or cleaning up a park in your neighborhood that you cannot stand seeing filthy. It can also be financial of course. There are a million ways to feel like a millionaire. Now turn the page and take the next step towards your greatness!

Step 1

RUN TOWARDS YOUR STORY, NOT FROM IT!

Repeat this affirmation as much as you need to:

>Today I give myself permission
>To no longer be a volunteer victim
>I will live life by my own rules
>And no longer listen to liars, haters, and fools
>I will take control of my own destiny
>And let no one get the best of me
>For if it is meant to be
>It is up to me!

My name is Omékongo Luhaka wa Dibinga wa Yenga Kakesse wa Tshintunkasa. For American cultural purposes, my first name is Omékongo and my last name is Dibinga. Writing my full name may be irrelevant to you but it means everything to me. You see, when I was growing up in Boston, Massachusetts in the 1970s and 80s, I was not allowed to say my name. Well, I could say my name, but chances were that it could lead to me being beaten up or at least verbally abused by my classmates and other neighborhood kids. Nowadays, however, I say my name with pride as a motivational speaker who inspires others to be more accepting of people of diverse backgrounds!

Do you know what it feels like to have just the mere mention of your name trigger violence? If not, maybe you will after reading part of my story. I am the 7th of 9 children. I was born in Cambridge, Massachusetts to Congolese parents. My parents escaped a very tumultuous situation in the Congo and made their way to America where they received nine academic degrees including three doctorates from Harvard and the Sorbonne. Sounds as if I should have had it easy growing up right? Well I did and I didn't. My life has been one of eternal dualities. I've been a have and a have-not, and I have been rich and poor at the exact same time.

In addition to being activists for Congolese independence and democracy, my parents were deep into the Black Power movement of the 1970s, thus they ended up leaving their teaching positions at Harvard and Boston College. With this, my family fell on tough times. Part of my elementary and middle school years were spent living a meager lifestyle in Roxbury, Massachusetts. During the winters, it sometimes got so cold in our house since we didn't have heat that we had to gather around the stove and cover ourselves over it with a blanket in order to keep warm. My friends used to joke during the winter about leaving our house to go outside where it was warm! I know what you're thinking—"some friends" right?

Our house was also infested at one point with rats and cats (don't know how they managed to get along in my house) who would enter from large holes on the side of our house. We also at times had neither electricity nor phone service. Lastly, there were frequent issues with the plumbing, leading us to have to boil water to take warm bucket baths or just take cold baths.

    The aforementioned situations would normally be enough to fracture the toughest child's spirit but this was not my only problem. Remember my name? Our names caused us to be tormented outside of our house. On the lighter side, my name became the subject of nursery rhyme remixes. "Old McDonald had a farm" became "Omékongo had a farm." On the darker side, we were beaten up and called all types of names like "African bush boogie" and "African booty scratcher." One of my more geographically challenged class-less-mates once called me a "Haitian booty scratcher."

    Kids really grasped at anything for new insults to hurl our way. On a deeper physical level, my eldest brother Said was even shot in the eye. One of his earliest memories of living in Boston is watching my older sister Shaumba pulling my two older brothers (Kabongo and Pata) by the hand back from school while "class"mates were throwing rocks at them and calling them names.

    Not only did our names make us stand out but so did our lack of designer clothes, which other students always noticed. A popular song back then for low priced shoes (called Bobos) we often heard was (sing along if you choose):

> *Bobos, they cost $1.99*
> *Bobos, they make your feet feel fine!*

They didn't feel all that fine.

This was the life of a material have-not in Boston, Massachusetts. Thoughts of suicide leased permanent space in my psyche. In my desperation, I turned to the one source of pride that I could find—my name, ironically. In my quest for my identity, I realized that my name had strong historical roots. I asked my parents what it meant and they told me I was named after a great Congolese warrior who saved my grandfather's life as a child. My grandfather, Yenga Kakesse, was captured around the age of 15 under Belgian colonial rule. Being a teenager, it was quickly determined by his captors that they would receive nothing for his capture from their leaders. Omékongo Luhaka, however, would be a great catch!
Being a warrior with a great heroic reputation, Omékongo was captured and my grandfather released. They killed Omékongo but for whatever reason, they could not move his body. In those days, if you could not bring back a body, you would bring back an arm of the corpse as proof of the slaying and that is what they did. Fortunately, however, Omékongo did not die. He rose from his deep unconsciousness and returned back one-handed to our village to continue protecting our people.
I know this all sounds mythological but my father actually knew this man and thus gave me that name in hopes that I would be a warrior for humanity. With a name like that, I decided I could no longer hold my head down! As Niche said, once

you understand your "why" for living, you can endure almost any "how" so having discovered my "why," I felt ready to take on the world!

Feeling like I had nothing to visibly grasp for pride at this stage in my life, I reached back into my past. I started to tell myself that if I was named after a warrior, I must live as one. Furthermore, I remembered the words of our neighbor Mrs. Johnson. See, it has been said that if you hear a negative comment once, you have to hear the opposite positive comment 17 times to negate the negative comment. For this, I owe Mrs. Johnson a great deal. Rumor had it she was a soothsayer!

My mother told me that Mrs. Johnson told her that I was going to do great things. I could not figure out why she chose me over all the other children on the street, but I stopped trying to figure it out. I just started telling myself that I am destined for more than my current circumstance. Rather than picking up the guns and shoot back or pick up the bats and swing back at our detractors, I decided to pick up the pen and write back, not fight back.

At first, I began writing to simply express my frustration and not commit suicide, but I soon realized that my writings could serve as a tool to make others understand me. I figured that maybe if I could show those who hated us that we all laugh and cry in the same language and that our homes get just as dark when the electricity bills aren't paid, those who tormented us would understand us better and embrace us. I was right!

As others began to hear my story, they slowly realized that we had more in common than apart. Slowly, as dialogue increased, the disrespect decreased. As I said in the beginning, I've been rich and poor at the same time. Throughout my struggles, I've always had a rich culture to draw strength from, even when I didn't realize it. It reminds me of a story by Zig Ziglar about a man who became a millionaire once it was discovered there was oil under his house. Ziglar mentioned that the man was already a millionaire who just needed his millionaire potential brought to the surface. Though I was a material have-not, I always had a strong family unit to get me through the toughest of times and that helped me to feel like a millionaire on many occasions, like when my sister Muadi pleaded with me to not kill myself. Glad I listened!

    My experiences led me to realize that I needed to devote my life to bridging the divides between different cultures, focusing particularly on young people who have experienced what I have gone through or even worse. I have lived, worked or performed in 16 countries and my work has been televised in over 150 countries. More on that later but rest assured, this little kid with the funny name who was beaten up for saying his name is now making a living speaking about his name and understanding cultural diversity. It all works out in the end my friend, if you stay on your course. Read on to see what I did and how you can conquer your living nightmares and live your dreams!

    It was once said that what happens in you is more important than what happens around you or to you. My circumstances never broke me on the inside. I never let them define me and that's what you must do. You must define your circumstances before they not only define you but ultimately destroy you.

No matter what you are experiencing, if you are reading this right now, you have the power to change your direction. You may be saying "Well, he had a strong family and history and I don't so I can't do what he did." We are always more quick to point out our weaknesses as opposed to our strengths, according to the world-renowned motivational speaker Les Brown. Robert Schuller said that we look for millions of reasons why we can't do something when all we need is one reason why we can. You must reassess your life and simply decide to pay more attention to the good going on in your life and not the bad.

Maybe you have a church elder who has helped you survive. Maybe you have a child who you want to have a better life than you did. No matter what you have experienced, you have to find the Mrs. Johnson in your story and focus on that as you climb your self-defined ladder of success. Though her comment was extremely profound for me, it was added on to the massive supportreceived from my parents and my siblings. My family literally saved my life during my most trying times. You may not have blood relatives to support you in the way I did, but there is always something or someone to grasp on to if you look hard enough.

If you could just find the strength to focus on what's good in your life, the good will eventually take over. Steve Duncanson profoundly stated that life is a battle for territory. Once you stop fighting for what you want, what you don't want will automatically take over. Don't you want to live your best life? If you really do, put on your boxing gloves and fight the beautiful struggle for your fabulous future! If it is meant to become true, it is up to you. As Brown says, stop being a volunteer victim and get out of your own way! The new you starts today!

The exercise below is designed to help you begin processing your past as you prepare for your future. Really take the time needed to analyze your history so that your future can be prosperous.

Exercise: What or who have been major obstacles in your life?

1. _____
2. _____
3. _____
4. _____
5. _____

G.R.O.W. Towards Your Greatness!

Who or what has been a major source of inspiration in your life?

1. _____

2. _____

3. _____

4. _____

5. _____

What's good for you in your life right now?

1. _____

2. _____

3. _____

4. _____

5. _____

What can you do to focus more on the positive aspects of your life?

1. _____
2. _____
3. _____
4. _____
5. _____

I intentionally did not write a section here for you to discuss the bad things in your life because we focus on them too much. There will be time to do some of that later. Remember, you are reading this book because you want to grow forwards, not backwards!

Step 2

ASK FOR WHAT YOU WANT OUT OF LIFE!

"All you need is already inside you! Just do it!"
-Nike

I am always amazed by what we are afraid to ask for in life. In fact, by our daily actions, we actually call into our lives the things we don't want out of life! We spend our time lamenting about what we do not have in our life. Just go through the day and count how many times you hear (or say):

"I don't have enough money."

"I don't have the right degree."

"I'm too short."

"I'm too fat."

"I'm too old."

"I'm too young."

"I'm too dark."

"I'm too light."

"I'm a former convict."
Is the list not endless? Before I go further, let me just respond to some of those daily negative affirmations we say to ourselves:

- ***"But I'm too young!"*** President Barack Obama's speech writer was 27 years old in 2008. He's been Obama's speech writer since he was 23! Most speeches you heard during his campaign were written by John Favreau, including parts of Obama's inaugural address

- ***"But I'm a former convict!"*** Charles S. Dutton, the famous actor and star of TV shows like Roc was a convicted felon

- ***"No one will hire me because of my past drug addiction!"*** Actor Samuel Jackson was a crack addict

- ***"I grew up poor!"*** Oprah Winfrey grew up in the segregated south and dealt with a massive range of family issues from abuse to poverty

- ***"I'll never have enough money!"*** Walt Disney filed for bankruptcy seven times and was even institutionalized at one point

- ***"But I have a disability!"*** Hee Ah Lee is a world-renown pianist from Korea who was born without legs and only two fingers on each hand and Dustin Carter is a wrestling star with no limbs

- **The writer of the hit song "Feliz Navidad,"** José Feliciano was born permanently blind and was told he should make a career begging for change

- **"But I was abused!"** Eve Ensler survived being sexually assaulted and is now a global advocate for rape victims

Do I really need to go further? Do I really have to mention that 80% of all millionaires have been financially bankrupt? Do I have to mention Stevie Wonder, Ray Charles, or Mattie Stepanek? How many examples do I have to give you of people who came from nothing or overcame obstacles as great or greater than yours in order to achieve their greatness? Maybe I'll tell you about one more person: Scott Hamilton.

Scott Hamilton was a 1984 Olympic gold medalist ice skater. This was a massive achievement by any means. However, Hamilton's personal story makes his achievement nothing more than remarkable. Hamilton spent much of his childhood in hospitals because of a rare digestive disease. He couldn't eat much and so he didn't grow like a normal child. At the age of 8, Hamilton looked like a 4-year old. When he first started skating, he had a feeding tube to accompany him on the ice.

By the age of 22, Hamilton was already placing in the Olympics. He then went on to win 16 consecutive world and national championships. He said his constant practice and commitment to the art helped him overcome his physical challenges, which he would really need later in life. Between 1997 and 2004, Hamilton was diagnosed with testicular cancer and a brain tumor and beat them both! He also found time to start Stars on Ice, which became larger than the Ice Capades (which he was fired from). You've probably seen a show!

Hamilton was not supposed to live into his teenage years. He now is over 50 and has a wife and two children. His philosophy on life is one we should all adopt:

"I believe if we just take a higher road, if we live as we're supposed to live, extraordinary things will happen for us."

Exercise: Are you living the way you're supposed to?

Take this time right now to write down what your ideal life would be like. Each page you turn in this book will help you get closer to that life if **you** let it!

_____

_____

_____

_____

_____

_____

G.R.O.W. Towards Your Greatness!

Step 3

ALWAYS REINVENT YOURSELF!

"Most people would rather die than change."
-Les Brown

      I would not have had as much success as I have if I was not willing to reinvent myself. Between March of 2006 and 2007, this poet has jumped into radio, rapping, and acting! I had no experience in radio as a broadcaster, but when the international satellite radio station WorldSpace came to me with the opportunity to host an international hip-hop show broadcasting in Asia, Europe, and Africa, I didn't say: "well I have no experience." I said: "when do I start?" They were willing to let me learn on the job and I did. I could not turn this opportunity down because one of my main goals in life is to let the world hear my voice so I can try to inspire others to live their best life. Given that, how could I blow the opportunity as long as I took the steps to learn?
      Many of the great personalities in life have become successful because they took chances, even when they were not necessarily prepared. When the opportunity presented itself, however,

these great people went into overdrive mode to prepare themselves! Will Smith was a Grammy award winning rapper who could have easily continued in that career. When he was offered the role on the new television show "The Fresh Prince of Bel-Air," Will Smith knew it was time to get prepared!

Smith spent days upon days watching television shows and movies to see what it is that actors do. He took classes and spoke to the greats. When the first show aired, you could see he was still a work in progress (he could be seen mouthing the words of the other actors because he memorized entire episode scripts), but today he is just the next film away from an Academy Award and has helped countless others get their start in film! He not only moved forward but he reached back and was instrumental in launching the film careers of actors such as Queen Latifah, Nia Long, Jamie Foxx and has his own movie production company called Overbrook.

I was also very comfortable as a poet but I knew if I wanted to reach more people, especially our youth, I had to start speaking in their language using hip-hop as well as increasing my overall media presence in general. Whether we like it or not, TV has become the new Ph.D. You are given more credibility with the increased media coverage you receive, even if you have no real knowledge of what you are speaking about. Just look at all of the reality show cast members who are now running for political office, shopping book deals, or getting their own television shows that promote nothing but sex,

G.R.O.W. Towards Your Greatness!

drugs, violence, or all three.

Rap superstar Kanye West actually was a painter before rapping, but said that his paintings did not speak loud enough to the people so rap became his platform. My story is similar. I started remixing the songs of rap artists like the late Tupac Shakur and Notorious B.I.G. just to show kids that they could sound like their favorite rappers without swearing or disrespecting women. I was also rapping as a child but I actually stopped because I was cursing so much and it took no creativity. That's why I turned to poetry because I was not mature enough to rap about positivity. Now I rap regularly and do poetry together at shows and it's great! I have released six CDs, some of them award-winning. Two of them were rap remakes. I now get requests from other countries for this music and I started out just wanting to show kids in my neighborhood a cleaner side of music!

My jump into acting has been incredible. In 2005, I was an extra for a Pepsi commercial, as well as an extra in a Disney movie called The Gameplan with wrestler-turned-actor Dwayne "The Roc" Johnson (another example of someone who reinvented himself). Musau, my sister and booking agent helped get my name and face out there. I also shot some short films with two of my filmmaker friends Safiya of Mpire Films and Gemal of Park Triangle Productions.

My big break came when my friend U-Meleni told me about a new show called "Ya Ma'Afrika," a show dealing with the lives of four African women living in Brooklyn, New York. This was to be a major TV drama series airing in North America on the Dish Network, as well as in Africa, Asia, Europe, and the West Indies! Should I have not even auditioned because I had not yet gone to acting school? What if Will Smith turned down The Fresh Prince of Bel-Air because he was not a trained actor? He was willing to reinvent himself and that is why whatever he touches turns to gold—or platinum multiple times over.

Having made the prior comments, I must also stress again the importance of preparation. It has been said that luck is when preparation meets opportunity. The late actress Lucille Ball originally was told she was a horrible actress. She ventured out and started her own show and now "I Love Lucy" is one of the most syndicated shows in television history. Ball once said: "The harder I work, the luckier I get." Feel lucky?

In this new mass media age that we live in, anyone with a blog is considered a journalist, even if he can't write or cannot back up his claims. Anyone who performs in front of the camera is called an actor, even if she can't act. The list goes on and on. As you continue to manage the coincidences in your life, you must make sure you are preparing yourself to be the best you can be in your chosen profession. You must listen to CDs, take classes, read, and just become a voracious consumer of information if you want to make a mark on the canvas of life.

One of my best examples of reinventing

myself comes from my experience in the speaking industry. Though I have been speaking for over 20 years, I am still new to the business of speaking. As I learned more about the profession, I started joining organizations like Toastmasters International and the National Speakers Association (NSA). Going to NSA conventions, working with Les Brown, reading books, and listening to audio recordings have helped me manage my coincidences. The best example of this is when I attended my first NSA convention in Phoenix. Just by walking around at the lunch table, I met a man who heads the Professional Speakers Association in Holland. A few weeks later, I was invited to speak at the PSA conference in Holland!

Seth Godin said in his book Tribes: we need you to lead us, that being good is no longer good enough so why not be great? Just because many around us have lowered their standards in so many areas does not mean that you have to! As Brown says, you must do the things today that others won't do, so you can have the things tomorrow that others won't have. This is why you must get started today! Brown also says that you don't have to be great to get started, but you have to get started to be great!

You have to get out of your own way and stop holding yourself back from opportunities. You already have enough detractors praying for your downfall. Don't become your own worst enemy. You have to embrace the opportunity to change whenever the chance presents itself. If you choose to stay the same, you choose to not grow!

Exercise: Get out of your own way!

Write down all the things you've always wanted to do but you convinced yourself not to!

1. _____
2. _____
3. _____
4. _____
5. _____

Write down the things you still want to do before your time is up (this can include items from part 1 of this exercise). This list is intentionally longer!

1. _____
2. _____
3. _____
4. _____
5. _____

6. _____

7. _____

8. _____

9. _____

10. _____

If you believe enough in yourself, you can and will find a way to make this list a reality if you just choose to reinvent yourself!

Step 4

VALUE YOURSELF AND YOUR WORK!

"I'd rather fail doing something I love than succeed doing something I hate."
-George Burns

    I have been writing for over 20 years. I have never taken a formal class on poetry, nor have I taken a class on public speaking. These things just come naturally to me so I honestly took it for granted because I love it so much. I just assumed that everyone could just get on stage at any age and talk in front of thousands of people. Because of this, when I started going to poetry venues, I never asked for payment for my services. I took whatever the venue would give, which was often nothing. I always looked at these venues as doing me a favor by letting me perform!
    Though I was doing what I loved, I did not develop a strong business mindset. I also felt that I didn't really need the money because I was always working a full-time job. I focused more on selling CDs than getting paid. I had some experiences asking for money when I did shows at colleges, for example. I learned that poets are treated like birthday clowns. We're told things like:

G.R.O.W. Towards Your Greatness!

"Well, we have a fashion show and have to pay for food so we can't pay for poets."
"We don't have a budget for poetry."
"We can't pay you but we can let you sell your product."

II accepted this for a while until I realized that the poets were always the highlight of any college event I attended. The rappers and singers were always hard to hear over their music. The food was never that great. The dances often focused more on revealing body parts than actual quality choreography. The fashion shows were fun, but did not leave most audience members feeling empowered.

As a poet with no band and no set rhyme pattern, all I had was my voice and my message so I had to deliver it as passionately as possible. Without fail, my fellow poets and I were always told that we were the highlight of the entire event. I had to ask myself: "Why are poets the most praised but the least paid?" I had to rethink my strategy.

As I got closer to quitting my job, I had to think about how much I could realistically make as a performer. I began slowly raising my fees to see what I could command. I heard the same comments as before, but I was steadfast in my terms. Motown legend Susan de Passe once said that we should make "no" our vitamin. That means that we should swallow every "no" we hear every day in order to give us the power to get closer to a "yes." Negotiations were also tough, and the advent of HBO's Def Poetry Jam, made it difficult for many of us to get what we wanted because we did not have the fortune of appearing on the show. The majority of the time, however, I won on my demands!

I was so confident that I could command what I wanted, that when I quit my job, I immediately raised my fees from hundreds of dollars to thousands of dollars. I attended a conference with the Publisher's Marketing Association where one speaker said: "Your clients will value you more if you cost more to book because clients do believe they'll get what they pay for." Andrew Morrison of The Small Business Camp said: "If you can get paid $1,000 for your work, you can get paid $100,000 for your work." If I ran into any problems with those who did not want to meet my fees, I asked the simple question: "How do I eat?" I showed my clients that I valued my work and deserved what I believed to be top dollar for it.

You have to look in the mirror and ask yourself: "If I don't value my work, who will?" You have to remember—you are a public speaker. You are a singer. You are an engineering consultant. You are a business. You have to think like one. Would there have been a Def Poetry Jam if HBO and Russell Simmons didn't think they could make money off of it?

In learning to value my work, I realized that without Def Poetry Jam, my work has still been televised in over 150 countries within the first 2 years of my starting to perform full time. I have performed directly in 7 countries. I also have a very strong academic background, which influences much of my work. I make myself desirable as a poet and, more recently, as a motivational speaker because of my academic and cultural background, my passionate delivery, my international experience (lived in, performed in, or visited 16 countries to date), and the ability to communicate to all ages and races in three languages—English, French, and Swahili.

  Does this sound like your story? Have you felt undervalued by your job or even family members? What is it that allows you to not value your work? What is it that makes you keep going back to that job or that abusive relationship? What is it that makes you sleep on your greatness? What is causing you to keep succeeding at something you hate? I would love to be on Def Poetry Jam if there is ever another season, but I told myself that I couldn't wait for someone else to validate me and you must have that same philosophy.

  As you read this, you may be working at a 9-5 job. How many times have you told yourself that you could do the job of your supervisor better than he could? How many times have you attended an "Employee of the month" ceremony and felt that you should be the one being honored? How many times have you trained someone on the job who times have youtrained someone onthe job who ended up advancing ahead of you? If any of these questions apply to you, my question is simple: if you know that you are more skilled in your profession than your boss and believe you are more capable than any of your co-workers, why are you not working for yourself or preparing yourself to do so? Could the reason be fear? More on that later!

Exercise: "Anything you can do I can do better!"
Write down anything you feel you can do better than your boss:

1. _____
2. _____
3. _____
4. _____
5. _____

Now write down why you're not doing it

6. _____
7. _____
8. _____
9. _____
10. _____

Write the potential <u>risks</u> of becoming your own boss

1. _____
2. _____
3. _____
4. _____
5. _____

Write the potential benefits of becoming your own boss

1. _____
2. _____
3. _____
4. _____
5. _____

After doing this exercise, I only have one question: are you willing to give up the good for the great?

Step 5

KEEP YOUR FRIENDS CLOSE, AND YOUR ENEMIES FAR AWAY!

"Know who you can count on and who you can count out!"
-John-Leslie Brown

    The cliché says that you should keep your friends close and your enemies closer. That is one of the most ridiculous things I have ever heard! Life is short. Why in the world would I want to surround myself with people who hate me and want me to fail? If you are trying to take yourself seriously, you need to surround yourself with people who take you seriously and will build your self esteem. This is true for your personal life as well as your business life. As I said before, it takes you 17 times to hear the positive opposite of a negative comment until you actually believe the positive comment to be true. I don't know about you, but I don't have that kind of time!

    My friends support and motivate me. I have a few friends that I've known since elementary and middle school. One of them, Richard, would always come to my shows and tell me: "O (my nickname), you're one of the best poets out there." He would tell me that every time he saw me perform. I always just smiled and thanked him for the compliment until I realized that he actually wasn't just saying it out of friendship, but that he actually thought I was among the best. Imagine what I would have begun to believe if he told me I was horrible every time he saw me perform and I kept inviting him to the shows?

When I was seriously thinking of quitting my job before I started Free Your Mind Publishing, I had a conversation with another best friend, Malik. Rather than tell me I should be more concerned with job security and my family, he said: "Well, you've always been known to make good decisions." You need that type of confidence and support from friends if you plan to venture out on your own and into the realm of entrepreneurship or if you just want to have a better quality of life overall.

Simply put, you will be much more successful if you have the support of your friends, your significant other, your spouse and other family members. I am fortunate to say that my parents and my siblings have always been supportive of my work. My parents always found opportunities to put me in the public eye to share my work or the work of others like Dr. Maya Angelou. Through my sister Shaumba's nonprofit organization, OrigiNation, I was always able to share my work at her dance recitals. The list goes on and on.

Lastly, I have been so fortunate to have the support and blessings of my wife Kendra in my personal life as well as in this business. We had been dating since 1994. She knew my aspirations of going to college to study international affairs and maybe

Look at anyone who is not helping you to reach your goals as the enemy and get as far away from them as possible. They will knowingly and often unknowingly bring you down. There is a reason why there are only a small number of billionaires in this world. They have a vision that no one else sees until they make it a reality. Anyone who sees things differently from them is considered a liability. If Amway's Dexter Yager still committed himself to hanging with his fellow beer truck drivers, he may have been content, but he would not be a billionaire with Amway. Remember also that Thomas Edison and Henry Ford were friends! Think they didn't push each other directly or indirectly? Watch the company you keep. As a matter of fact, start now! Write down who you can count on and who you can count out and start counting today! Writedownwhoyoucancountonandwhoyou can countoutand startcountingtoday!

Exercise: "You can count on me!"
Who can you count <u>on</u> and why?

1. _____

2. _____

3. _____

4. _____

5. _____

6. _____

7. _____

8. _____

Who can you count out and why?

1. _____

2. _____

3. _____

4. _____

5. _____

6. _____

7. _____

8. _____

If you have more people on list #2 than you do on list #1, you have some work to do in order to detoxify your life!

Step 6

PERFECTION IS PROCRASTINATION!

"The thing that is really hard, and really amazing is giving up on being perfect and beginning the work of becoming yourself."
-Anna Quindlen

I attended a business conference where undergraduate and graduate students had an opportunity to enter a business plan competition. As I watched the great presentations take place, I was kicking myself for not having my business plan ready. The presenters in the competition were great and extremely motivational. I may not have won the competition, but I know I could have at least been competitive. Why did I not have my business plan ready? It was due to a sad case of PPD—Perfection & Procrastination Disorder.

I spent so much time trying to fine tune my work that I was nervous about presenting it. It was a few days after the conference that I heard a quote that said "anything worth doing is worth doing badly." What this means is that if you're going to attempt something, don't just do it because you're comfortable in that zone. You have to be willing to go out and embarrass yourself in order to get what you need. Robert Kiyosaki, the author of Rich Dad, Poor Dad calls it the "Jim Carrey" or "Dumb & Dumber" effect—the dumber Jim Carrey acts, the more he gets paid! Don't be afraid to look like a fool as long as you are prepared to improve!

    I should have entered the competition with my imperfect plan. I would have had an opportunity to have very successful businesswomen and men look at my work and critique it. I don't mind critique, but I was taught through schooling to never give a copy to someone that isn't my best quality, even if it's a rough draft. This does not work in entrepreneurship. You have to be willing, as Brown said, to "fail forward." Be willing to go out and fail from your efforts in order to reach your goals.

    Needless to say, I finished my business plan within two weeks of that event, but the competition would have allowed me to receive more attention from potential investors to Free Your Mind Publishing, because it would have allowed me to do what I do best—speak in front of people. In business, as long as your ideas are protected in the form of copyrights, trademarks, patents, etc., you should be willing to put your work in front of as many supportive people and organizations as possible until you reach your short term goals. If you hold on to or for something for too long, you may blow your opportunity or even lose motivation in your project. Tell yourself never again!

    Make a list right now of what you've been putting off and when you will get it done! Commit to getting constructive feedback along the way!

Exercise: The Cure to PPD

1. Project #1: _____

   Progress to date: _____

   What is needed for completion:_____
   _____

   Completion date: _____

2. Project #2: _____

   Progress to date: _____

   What is needed for completion:_____
   _____

   Completion date: _____

3. Project #3: _____

   Progress to date: _____

   What is needed for completion:_____
   _____

   Completion date: _____

4. Project #4: _____

   Progress to date: _____

   What is needed for completion:_____
   _____

G.R.O.W. Towards Your Greatness!

   Completion date: _____

5. Project #4: _____

   Progress to date: _____

   What is needed for completion:_____

   _____

   Completion date: _____

    Willie Jolley is the world's leading motivational speaker, singer, and author. He once said that success can be your biggest failure. He was once a very successful jazz singer in Washington, DC. He had won several Wammies, which is the DC area's version of the Grammy award. Jolley said that he was regularly selling out nightclubs and was basically "the man." It was for these reasons that when his boss called him in for a meeting, he thought it was for some type of promotion. Well it was and it wasn't.

    The club manager told Jolley that even though he was great with his band, the club needed to cut costs. They decided to replace Jolley and his band with a karaoke machine! Jolley couldn't believe it. He went home and told his wife that he was tired of other people determining his destiny. Slowly but surely, he made his way into motivational speaking and makes tens of thousands of dollars an hour around the globe. He says that sometimes he wants to go back and thank the manager for firing him because had he not been fired, he would not have realized that there were greater days ahead of him. He was so comfortable in his prior success that he was not interested in giving up the good in order to go for the great!

Are you willing to give up the good in order to go for the great? Are you the next Willie Jolley? Better yet, are you the first you? Are you paying rent in your comfort zone when you could be paying a mortgage on the success home of your dreams? Would you accept me saying "congratulations" to you if you told me you were fired today? Dr. Maya Angelou said that we drive to a certain point on the highway of life and just park because it is the comfortable place to be. Get out of dodge!!!

STEP 7

LEARN MONEY MANAGEMENT

"Money isn't the most important thing in life, but it's reasonably close to oxygen on the 'gotta have it' scale."
-Zig Ziglar

I believe in what Dr. Farrah Gray said. If you do not know Dr. Gray, all you really need to know is that he came up from a tough neighborhood in the south side of Chicago and became a millionaire at the age of 14! He said that when choosing a career, you should find something that you would do for free if we lived in a world where we didn't need money. That is where you will find your career. Brown says do what you would do for free so well that others will pay you for it. It would be remiss of me to speak about choosing your path to greatness and pursuing your dreams without speaking briefly about money management.

I don't know how many times I've heard an artist say "I'm just in this for the love. I just wanna perform." I used to be that person and I still am to a degree. But my belief now is that if you love what you do, you should be able to get paid and save money so that you can do more of what you love. This won't happen unless you get your financial house in order.

A report on CNN in 2006 said that a large percentage of college graduates in the new millennium are graduating without the ability to balance a check book! And where exactly are the soaring costs of tuition going???!! The concern for me is that if college graduates are graduating financially illiterate, what are our artists and those without college degrees who don't study business doing financially? What are you thinking of financially? Can you manage your money?

If you want to get paid, you need to learn to manage your money—like yesterday. If you value your work as we spoke about before, you have to be able to create stock of your products (if you create product), manage the revenue stream, and be willing to outsource skills you don't have in order to build your enterprise.

Using myself as an example, I've struggled mightily with tracking product sales over the years. I've lived between three different cities and I kept inventory in each place in case I traveled back there for performances. The problem was that whenever I would do a show, I would not count the amount of products I brought to the show. I would frantically try to write down the number of sales as they were taking place, but as the lines grew, I would lose track. At the end of the shows I would have pockets full of cash, checks, and credit card receipts, and have no idea what I sold! I would only know how much I made and not always entirely because I would mix the amount of change I brought (which I never counted) in with the money I was making. Great accounting, right?

If you're selling multiple products like I do (T-shirts, CDs, books, and DVDs), you need to know what's selling so you can keep a fresh inventory. This is the case if you sell paintings, books, gift-baskets, etc. Record your inventory before and after a show or event. Keep your change separate from the money you collect from sales and count it! Get software like QuickBooks that can help you set up a proper accounting system. If you get an accountant to help you, make sure they are helping, not running your company. You still need to watch your books! This is not just the case in business but in your personal life as well.

One of the best ways that this is demonstrated in our personal lives is with our bank accounts. Referring back to the CNN report, many students who are graduating from college today do not know how to balance a checkbook. At the same time, these students are being offered a credit card on the first day of college as long as they buy a pizza or T-shirt. When I was younger, I took advantage of these offers too.

I'll admit, I didn't always pay close attention to my bank balance. Once I started working on getting a house, however, I had to pay more attention to my credit history and monitored every transaction. I figured it's better for me to know what's going on with my account and my credit instead of being told at a mortgage company while I'm trying to apply for a mortgage! You must do the same!

The great motivational speaker and author Iyanla Vanzant has experienced financial despair even after achieving stardom. Her books have been bestsellers. I recently saw her on a panel where she boldly confessed to the shocked audience and the entire world watching that she lost her house in 2006 and also did not have health insurance. She got caught in a mortgage she didn't understand and it cost her dearly. Her message was that you can't have someone else in charge of your financial house. It is only up to you! As Kiyosaki says, many financial brokers will only make you "broker" in the end. Handle your financial business!

You must also learn how to save your money. I can't remember how many times I went out to eat or party after a show and blew some of my new-found income on a night on the town. I couldn't wait for more in-come to come-in! I didn't pay myself first, which many businessmen advocate. When all of the talking is done and all of the new year resolutions are made, at the end of the day you are what you eat and you are what you spend your money on. Warren Buffet said the best thing he ever spent money on or invested in was himself, not the stock market or material items. You must develop that mentality.

Lastly, after you develop an appreciation for getting, saving, and spending money, you cannot become attached and consumed by it. You must learn money management but don't let your money manage you. Ziglar says that it's great to have all the things money can buy but we must first concentrate on having the things money can't buy. He states that money can buy you a big house, but it can't buy you a home. It can buy a big bed, but it can't buy you a good night's sleep. Lastly, he says, it can buy you a spouse, but it can't buy you a mate. We have seen so many celebrities squander their lives away with their money because they did not first have the character to sustain them when they received the fame and what turned out to be misfortune.

Exerci$e: It'$ all about the Benjamin$!

Write down what you need to do in order to better manage your finances. You may need to complete this exercise with a neutral partner or financial planner who can better assess your situation. Extra space is provided because we spend too much time not talking about our finances!

_____

_____

_____

_____

_____

_____

G.R.O.W. Towards Your Greatness!

Step 8

MAKE SACRIFICES!

"The hardest thing to learn in life is which bridge to cross and which to burn."
-David Russell

You must be willing to make sacrifices if you want to reach your goals. Many people want the cheap way out. In this microwave society we live in, we want everything now. Just zap it and it'll appear, even if we really haven't defined what "it" is. The advent of reality shows and instant stardom from MySpace, Facebook, and YouTube have added to this phenomenon. I mean, why go to school if you can make it to American Idol or The Apprentice and get stardom overnight? We just want to get over in too many ways without putting in real effort.

Nowadays, we are quick to cut corners on just about anything and we rarely want to pay for what we think we want. When I started to put my first book together, From the Limbs of my Poetree, I was willing to do whatever it took in order to say I was a published author, but not at the expense of lowballing anyone. Gemal Woods of Park Triangle Productions said it wonderfully: "If I tell a client that I will charge them $1 for a project, he will always ask me if he can pay $0.75." So many people want to just get over. If you want to reach your goals, you can't just get over and be haphazard about your goals. Show people that you respect them as well as your dream well enough to pay them what they're worth!

Remember, I started working on my first book right as I was quitting my job. I did not have the funds to pay outright for my printing costs. Did I ask the printer for discounts or handouts? No. I began selling things in my apartment like exercise equipment in order to get the funds I needed. This was how bad I wanted to be published. How bad do you want "it"?

Now that my company is established, I run into many people who do not have that same passion. When I tell them FYMP's pricing, I get story after story of how poor people are, how they're on a fixed income, or how we can work out a "hook up." My response is often: "Does this 'hook up' pay my mortgage? Does this 'hook up' feed my daughters?" If the answer is "NO", there is nothing to discuss. When I am making deals on new products, I present my subcontractors with what I can do and what I cannot do. If they cannot work within my means, I move on. It is in my and their best interest to do so.

One of the other mistakes we make about sacrifices is that we always see sacrifice as a bad thing. We always look at it based on what we have to give up as opposed to what we're gaining. Below is an exercise that Les Brown talks about in his book, It's Not Over Until You Win! The goal of the exercise is to not only realize what you have to do to accomplish your goals, but also what you will have to give up in order to reach your goals, without the "hookup."

When doing this exercise, really think long and hard about it. Maybe you are willing to give up eating out five times a week but missing your child's recitals is an absolutely must do. Maybe you will only go out with your spouse once a week and make the 2nd night you usually go out a work-in session where you build your vision. It's generally easy to decide between the first option on eating out vs. your child's recitals, but the second set of choices is where it will start to get difficult. Are you willing to miss your child's graduation for a speaking engagement that will air on local television and earn you thousands of dollars? Write down your non-negotiables now and stick to them! Rip them out of this book if you need to and post them somewhere where you will always see them!

Exercise #: Goals

What will you need to do to accomplish your goals?

1. _____

2. _____

3. _____

4. _____

5. _____

6. _____

7. _____

8. _____

9. _____

10. _____

What will you have to give up in order to accomplish your goals?

1. _____

2. _____

3. _____

4. _____

5. _____

6. _____

7. _____

8. _____

9. _____

What are your non-negotiables?

1. _____

2. _____

3. _____

4. _____

5. _____

6. _____

7. _____

8. _____

9. _____

10. _____

STEP 9

QUIT YOUR JOB TODAY!

"I've been too chicken...afraid to live my life, so I sold it to you for $300 freaking dollars a week!"
-Tom Hanks, Joe vs. the Volcano

    As you know, we are living through one of the worse economic periods this country has seen in years. Millions of homes are being lost to foreclosure. Hundreds of thousands of jobs have been lost. Families are committing murder-suicides because of the bills. The list goes on and on.
    My own family has suffered during these times as well. At the time of this writing, my wife and I have limited savings. We have two children under four years old. We are carrying two mortgages, two car notes, student loan balances and still have credit card debt. It is for all of these reasons that I quit my job today.
    This sounds backwards doesn't it? Why would I quit a good paying job when so many others are losing theirs? The answers are simple. First off, I reminded myself of an Oprah interview I saw. She said the best thing she ever did was invest in herself. The second best thing she did was invest in Dr. Phil. For some reason, I do not believe that Oprah and

Dr. Phil are struggling at this time of year. What I realized is that I could no longer spend my time making others successful at the expense of my own dreams and so I threw caution to the wind.

Les Brown said that we should look at every job as a paid internship. He said that every job will only use you to the best of their needs, not your own. You will be paid just enough to keep from quitting and you will work just hard enough to keep from getting fired. This is the case for most Americans. If I am wrong, then why do we say "Thank God it's Friday" as opposed to "Thank God it's Monday?" if I'm wrong, why do most heart attacks occur on Monday mornings before people go to work? It's simple: your heart is fighting you from going to a place that your mind has convinced you that you need and so it attacks you. You have to ask yourself: is it worth it? I decided it was not.

I decided that I could not continue with my job. There was a great deal of disrespect and lack of support that was occurring from my supervisors though I was giving more than 100% and my peers were giving me evaluations as good or better than other colleagues in my position. I was driving 73 miles a day at the height of the gas price hike. An hour long commute took two hours plus on some days because of traffic. I was missing valuable time with my growing daughters. Lastly, though I was making decent money, we were not making any serious advancement towards financial freedom. It was time to go.

I once heard the word job described as the **j**ourney **o**f the **b**roke. Kiyosaki says that wimp stands for "**W**here **i**s **m**y **p**aycheck?" Regardless of what acronyms one uses, the fact is the same—you will never achieve riches financially or spiritually as long as you continue to work for someone else. Don't get me wrong. If you're a teacher who can't wait until Monday because you can't wait to inspire hopeful students, then you've found your calling and riches isn't your goal. If you're a nurse and nothing pleases you more than healing the sick, keep healing! If you're a sanitation worker and you see your role in life as being the one who helps keep our streets clean, you have indeed found your calling. I am only speaking to the more than 80% of you who admittedly hate your jobs!

It has been said that we'd rather endure known hells as opposed to pursue unknown pleasures. Why stay in your comfort zone? Have you yet to realize, as Brian Tracy said, that your comfort zone is really your danger zone? As long as you stay in this zone, you're in danger of never achieving your dreams and unrealized dreams are living nightmares! Live your dreams!

Within two weeks of quitting my job, the world began to open its doors to me. I've since been invited to speak in the United Kingdom, and I have spoken in Senegal and Canada. I was invited to participate (all expenses paid) in Tavis Smiley's annual State of the Black Union Conference, and I boarded a plane for Disney World for the National Speaker's Association conference and I didn't have to fake any sick days to do it! Seth Godin put it best when asked: Rather than having a job that you have to get away from every year with a two-week vacation, why not create the type of job and life that you won't want to escape from?

What is also sad is that this is not the first time a job has shown a lack of appreciation for my contributions. I found out that another job I once had was cheating me out of $10,000 in my salary and also quickly realized that my supervisor would never allow me to surpass him. At the same time, my passion for speaking was calling me. I was being torn apart. Years later, I had the same problem and life coach Vince Toran told me clearly that this will keep happening as long as I keep going down the same path.

You must have the courage to be bold in this life because you are the only you the world will see. Whether your name is John or Amadou, Sally or Seynabu, there can only be one you. Others may have the same name as you, but they cannot play the same game of life that you do. When names like Mandela, Clinton, Washington, McCain, Obama, etc. are mentioned, everyone thinks of one person for that name and everyone else is secondary. Why are you not the first person others think of when they think of your name? It's because you have not unleashed your inner greatness!

We spend so much time trying to be like the biggest rock star, athlete, actor, or politician, that we forget to be the first us. We buy make-up like Beyoncé, try to sing like Sinatra, and so on. We are told in this world to be like everyone else but ourselves. Let me ask you one question: since there was no you before you and the world will not see another you after you, why not just be you? As motivational speaker Al McDougall says: "You have to be you! Everyone else is taken!" Whether you live in a mansion or a shack, whether you are white or black, you were meant to be exactly who you are. Whether you're tall enough that the sky you can touch or you move along in a wheelchair or on a crutch, you were not given any circumstance that you cannot handle. That's why you were chosen to experience what you are dealing with. Brown says it quite simply: "You've been picked out to be picked on!"

  Like it or not, you are being tested to see whether you can sink or swim. So swim, swim, swim! Swim towards your destiny! Swim towards your greatness! Don't swim towards someone else's greatness. You will never arrive there! It has been said that we are all born as originals, but we die as copies trying to be something we were never destined to be. If you truly want to be happy, be yourself! Pursue your dreams! If you quit your job today, you just became your own boss and hired a new you! Congratulations! If you were just fired or laid off, you've just been given permission by the universe to pursue your greatness!

Exercise: Dream in broad daylight!

Answer the following question: what would your life look like with your dreams realized?

_____
_____
_____
_____
_____
_____
_____
_____
_____

Has your life ever looked so beautiful?

Step 10

G.R.O.W.!

"The moment you become satisfied is the moment you will stop growing."
-Christina Pagliarulo

So we have finally come to step 10: "G.R.O.W." You've probably been asking all of this time, what does G.R.O.W. stand for? The reason why I saved this for last is because it is a simple phrase, but it says a great deal. Whenever you are encountering a problem that seems to be insurmountable, just tell yourself to G.R.O.W. Make sure you are always focused on G.R.O.W.ing forward and not going backwards. Let's break down the acrostic!

The **"G"** means give. One of the major differentiating characteristics of those who are successful and those who are not is the quality (not the quantity) of their giving. Brown gave an example of visiting an inner-city neighborhood and lamented the fact that this particular project complex received a $100,000 beautification grant. He told the city representative that it shouldn't take a grant to make someone go to the store, buy a bottle of disinfectant and clean up a urine-soaked hallway, especially if a tenant was the one doing the urinating!

I have seen similar examples of the aforementioned case everywhere I travel. Earl Nightingale, known to many as the "Dean of personal development," once said that we're all self-made but only the successful will admit it. Many who are not that successful actually walk around with a sense of entitlement and complain about what the government owes them. These people fail to realize that the more they give the more they will receive as opposed to demanding more and receiving less.

Ed Foreman says that you can have everything you want in this life as long as you first help others get what they want. Wayne Dyer says that the more and more you take from the universe, the more and more it is going to take from you. Conversely, the more you give to the universe, the more it will give back to you. Everyone from Oprah to Donald Trump speak to this truth. You may not be able to give $1,000,000 to your favorite organization or school, but you can start something as simple as a street beautification project. In many cases, being more giving of your personal time is better than any financial gift you can make. The fact of the matter is, the more you give, the more you get. As you remember from my story, the more I opened up in my community, the more people opened up to me!

The **"R"** stands for release! Let it go, whatever IT is. The strongest example of this is found with the idea of forgiveness. Mark Twain once said that forgiveness is the fragrance that the violet leaves on the heel that has crushed it. Have you forgiven someone who has done you wrong today? One thing that many of us fail to realize is that forgiveness is more important for the person doing the forgiving than the person who is being forgiven. It is you who must release the tension in your body keeping you from advancing.

  Robert Muller said "to forgive is the highest, most beautiful form of love. In return, you will receive untold peace and happiness." Who do you need to forgive today? Who is preventing you from getting to a higher level? You know what's so sad? The person who you refuse to forgive is probably somewhere having a good time! While you're at home having a pity party, they're out really partying or at the game and not even thinking about you! Don't give them any more power over you than they've already had!

  At the end of the day, you have to ask yourself, as Marlo Thomas said, do you want to stay bitter or become better? Do you prefer to get even or get ahead? Life doesn't care about your excuses, only your results, so let it go! Whether I'm talking about larger issues like enslavement or the Holocaust or personal issues such as abuse you may have suffered, you have to move on for your own sake. Now I'm not saying you have to become friends with these people. I don't expect you to go out and have some tea. What I am saying is to do what you need to do in order to not let those who did you wrong in the past have any power over you. You are too important to spend time living in the past. Use the past as a place of reference, not residence, as Willie Jolley says.

Inspirational author Catherine Ponder said it best when she said: "When you hold resentment toward another, you are bound to that person or condition by an emotional link that is stronger than steel. Forgiveness is the only way to dissolve that link and get free." Don't you want to be free today? Find out what it's like and whether you choose to forget or not, you must forgive. If not, you will never forgive yourself for not becoming the best you can be. Remember the word "forgiving" means "for giving"; for giving yourself permission to move on. I can't even remember the names of most of the bullies and detractors my family has had. I forgave them. Release the pain and G.R.O.W. forward!

The **"O"** stands for overcome. Once you release, you have to demonstrate to yourself and others that you have moved on and have become a better person. You have to confront your pain or your fears head on and prove to yourself that your circumstances won't define you, but you will define them. This could manifest itself in several ways.

One of the best ways to illustrate this example is with families. In most families, there is always some lingering issue between a parent and a sibling, a sibling and a sibling, or the parents themselves. I remember speaking to one of my friends who told me that the way her father abused her caused her to have issues dealing with men. She became promiscuous and could not keep a serious relationship, partially because she had never seen one. She was heading towards disaster.

As she became older and had a child from yet another failed relationship, she began to become really self-reflective. Determined to not let her daughter grow up like she did, she sought assistance from a psychologist, and she also began paying more attention to the girlfriends she wrote off who were always telling her she deserved better and was a queen inside. The more she continued with her therapy and the more she let the positive people back into her life, the more her self esteem grew.

Her biggest step in overcoming was to forgive her father for his actions, which she did. She is now in a great relationship, has a wonderful career, and her child is seeing a positive family, which she will hopefully seek to emulate. She overcame and so can you if you surround yourself with the right people. Brown says that you should ask for help not because you are weak, but because you want to remain strong.

The **"W"** stands for win. You have to develop a winning mentality. Once you overcome your particular predicament, you must now take that success mindset to every other aspect of your life. This is what millionaires do. Eighty percent of millionaires have declared bankruptcy at some point. The women and men often fail, but they've developed a winning formula that allows them to regenerate income and get back to the top in no time.

G.R.O.W. Towards Your Greatness!

    I used to have a fear of flying. I was like the late Bea Arthur in an episode of the Golden Girls. Her character, Dorothy, was afraid of flying but she had to get on a plane with her housemates. When one tried to speak to her, she told her: "Don't look at me when you speak! It'll shake the plane!" That was me 110%! The problem I had was that I made it my mission to make the world hear my voice and since everyone doesn't have a television around the world (much less cable), I had to figure out how to go to them!

    After a great deal of research, I realized it would take too long to boat around the world and speak so flying became my only option. To date, I have traveled to 16 countries and counting. As Dexter Yager said, if the dream is big enough, the problems don't matter. Though I haven't completely conquered my fear of flying (people can look at me when they talk to me now), I am confident that I will travel safely to my destination because I am contributing something to humanity so I feel as if I am working for and with the universe.

    The winning mentality that helped me conquer my fear of flying has transferred over into everything else I do. I had a fear of starting a business and throwing caution to the wind but I did it because the dream of helping more people and becoming financially secure is not an option for me. I was nervous about moving from renting to home ownership because it was foreign to me but now I own two homes. This winning mentality helped me go from reciting poetry to learning to be a positive rapper, then an actor, and now a motivational speaker. Once I fix my

G.R.O.W. Towards Your Greatness!

mind on something, it's just a matter of time in my eyes before I conquer it because I know it's not over until I win!

So there it is ladies and gentleman, G.R.O.W.:

Give
Release
Overcome
Win!

This formula will work for you in your personal as well as professional life. If you truly study anyone you admire, you will find that they have utilized this technique in some way, shape, or form. If it worked for them, it can work for you! You have greatness in your future but you have to accept it and prepare for it. No matter what station you find yourself in life, you can indeed G.R.O.W. towards your greatness! Write these steps down in a place that's easy to see! Say it or read it three times a day or more if you need to. Make it happen!

On the next page is a pictoral diagram of the G.R.O.W. model. The model was developed by my wife and graphically created by Stephanie Vance-Patience. It also appears as a perforated page in the back of this book. Blow it up and put it on your wall if you need to. As you'll see, growing is an iterative process with a singular goal—winning. You may be able to accomplish one of these principles in the circle in a different order than the spelling of the word "G.R.O.W." and that's fine! Just keep G.R.O.W.ing!

G.R.O.W. Towards Your Greatness!

    The delta or triangle symbol represents change. Once you've developed a winning mentality, you may suffer setbacks that may put you back to one of the other areas on your life raft of success but since you are focused on G.R.O.W.ing forward you will never commit to staying there. The car dealer Sewell said that once you make the commitment to be the best, the majority of your decisions are already made for you because everything you decide to do will be based on being the best! There's no turning back from that!

G.R.O.W.
Towards Your Greatness

Your winning strategy for personal and professional growth!

If this model helps you overcome a family matter, see if you can transfer it over to a problem you may have with a friend. If it is successful there, see if you can apply it to your professional life. Anyone or any company that has triumphed has used a similar philosophy. Oprah Winfrey serves as one of the best examples of this principle.

Oprah is very candid about her struggles growing up poor and running with the wrong crowd. When she went to go live with her father, her life started to become more disciplined. As she matured, she found the strength to forgive those who did her wrong. She also forgave herself for some of the things she did that she did not feel proud of. She didn't forget her past, but she released it from weighing her down. The more she began to give (way before the millions), the more society gave back to her. As she overcame her past, she grew stronger and stronger. Now her winning mentality has transferred from her personal life into the corporate world, to school creation, and beyond!

Exercise: Time to G.R.O.W.! No more excuses!

What can you do to give back to your community right now?

_____

_____

G.R.O.W. Towards Your Greatness!

DO IT!

What do you need to release in order to get on with your life??

LET IT GO!

What obstacles do you need to overcome?

G.R.O.W. Towards Your Greatness!

OVERCOME NOW!

What have you been successful in and how can you transfer that success into another area that you are scared to conquer?

_____
_____
_____
_____
_____

G.R.O.W. Towards Your Greatness!

Other products from Free Your Mind Publishing

From The Limbs Of My Poetree
Omékongo's first trilingual book of poetry!
Available for a limited time with a special edition, over 90-minute DVD!
$24.95

G.R.O.W. Towards Your Greatness!

Poems From The Future: Poetic Reflections From The Next Generation
Read the voices of Westland Middle School's Class of 2005!
$19.95

Put Your Shoes On! A Step-by-Step Guide for Youth Entering the Workforce
$14.95

G.R.O.W. Towards Your Greatness!

G.R.O.W. Towards Your Greatness! Listen to Omekongo's motivational messages set to music! Introduction by Les Brown!
$9.95

A Young Black Man's Anthem

**Omékongo's 1st spoken word CD!
Poetry in English, French, and Swahili!
Winner of the Cambridge Poetry Award for "Best CD"!
$14.95**

G.R.O.W. Towards Your Greatness!

Signs of the Time
Omékongo's 2nd spoken word CD! Poetry in English, French, and Swahili! Enhanced CD!
$14.95

Reality Show
Omékongo's first rap/spoken word hybrid CD
$14.95

G.R.O.W. Towards Your Greatness!

**Get your Free Your Mind Publishing T-shirts today in black, white, brown, blue, and orange! Baby-tees available in black, white, red, and green!
$14.95
Front of shirt**

G.R.O.W. Towards Your Greatness!

Quick Order Form

Fax orders: (202) 889-5056
Telephone orders: Call (202) 251-7746
Email orders: info@freeyourmindpublishing.com
Postal orders: Free Your Mind Publishing
PO Box 70 Boston, MA 02131, USA

Please send the following books, disks or reports.
_____
_____

Please send more FREE information on:
__ Other Products __ Speaking Engagements __Consulting
Name: _____
Address: _____
City: _____ State: _____ Zip: _____
Telephone (day) _____
   (evening) _____
Email: _____
___ Please add me to your e-mail mailing list!
Sales tax: Add 7.75% sales tax for products shipped to California addresses.

Shipping by air
U.S. $5.50 for first book, $4.50 for CD and shirts, and $2.50 for each additional product.

International: $9.00 for first book or disk; $5.00 for each additional product (estimate)

Payment: __Visa __Mastercard __Optima __AMEX __Discover
Card number: _____
Name on card: _____ Exp. Date: _____

"Opening eyes, one mind at a time."

www.ingramcontent.com/pod-product-compliance
Lightning Source LLC
Chambersburg PA
CBHW072103290426
44110CB00014B/1807